HOW TO U

Provides a full description of the Major and Minor Arcana, explanations of the meanings attached to the emblematic pictures of the Major Arcana, and a specimen reading from the 'Great Pack' of the combined Major and Minor Arcana.

HOW TO UNDERSTAND THE TAROT

by

FRANK LIND

THE AQUARIAN PRESS
Wellingborough, Northamptonshire

First published in this series 1969
Sixth Impression 1976
Second Edition, completely revised,
enlarged and reset, 1979
Third Impression 1983
Fourth Impression 1984
Fifth Impression 1986

ISBN 0 85030 177 7 (UK)
ISBN 0 87728 436 9 (USA)

Printed in Great Britain by
Richard Clay (The Chaucer Press),
Bungay, Suffolk.

CONTENTS

		Page
Foreword		7
Chapter		
1.	The Major Arcana	13
2.	The Minor Arcana	72
3.	Divination by the Tarot	83
	Index	93

FOREWORD

Symbolism may be defined as the mechanism by which we are able to mine the infinite riches buried deeply within universal consciousness. No man is an island and the accumulated wisdom of the ages is our common heritage. But how does one utilize this wisdom for counteracting the difficulties and problems of everyday life?

One answer is provided by the Tarot. A Tarot pack contains 78 cards, comprising the Minor and the Major Arcana. There are four suits of 14 cards each in the Minor Arcana. Unlike our modern playing card suits of diamonds, hearts, clubs and spades, the Tarot suits are made up of wands, cups, swords and pentacles (five-pointed stars). The Major Arcana consists of 22 trump cards, each bearing a symbolic picture.

The origins of the Tarot are lost in the mists of time, a fact that does not worry Frank Lind. He says: 'Whether the cards came from India, Egypt, or China, reached Italy first from the last-mentioned, were introduced into the West from the East by the Crusaders or Arabs, or arrived in Europe with the Gipsies, is of little moment. What is of far more importance than the age of the cards is the antiquity of much of their symbolism. As to this, at least, there can be no divergence of opinion.'

So we may as well content ourselves with an occult tradition that dates the origin of Tarot cards at *c*. A.D.1200. Yet, why were they invented? The occultists' explanation is that a centre for world-wide occultism was created at Fez in Morocco and the Tarot was developed there to overcome language barriers. Esoteric truths were thus enshrined pictorially in the Tarot.

Although a number of Tarot packs were produced in the nineteenth century (and more in the twentieth century), the pictures are by no means identical, nor do the explanations of the pictures agree in every particular. For example, in the Tarot pack designed by A.E. Waite, card number 6 in the Major Arcana – 'The Lovers' – depicts a man and a woman being united in marriage by a winged angel. But an older version (used by Frank Lind in this book) portrays a young man hesitating before the rival blandishments of two females representing Vice and Virtue.

Undoubtedly the most enigmatic Tarot trump is 'The Fool'. All the other cards in the Major Arcana are numbered – from 1 to 21 – but 'The Fool' has a 'zero' value. This card shows a young, carefree man walking briskly, although he is within inches of the edge of a precipice. Over his right shoulder he carries a small bundle suspended from a stick. A small dog frolics around his feet. (In the Waite pack he also holds a flower instead of the more traditional staff of an older version). The young man's gaze is directed heavenwards: he is oblivious of the dog and the yawning chasm in front of him.

Directly contradicting the world's much-vaunted 'wisdom', 'The Fool' proclaims that folly is trumps. (Since the dawn of Christianity there have been mystics and visionaries who have accounted it a privilege to be regarded as fools for the sake of Christ). Relative to the symbolism of 'The Fool's' small bundle, Frank Lind comments: 'The bundle contains not only all his worldly possessions, of which he needs but few, but it may be taken to be the sum-total of all his past experiences, which in his estimation really amount to nothing.'

Each card of the Minor and the Major Arcana has its own meaning: instructions for interpretation will be included with any Tarot pack one may buy. But the student should not expect cut-and-dried answers in the manner of an oracle. Tarot symbols are meant to be meditated upon, and then various meanings will appear, depending upon the understanding of the individual.

Like the science of astrology the Tarot can be used for fortune telling but to do this is to debase its transcendent significance. The Ancient Greek injunction 'know thyself' is capable of reaching its supreme fulfilment in us through a dedicated search for the eternal truths hidden in the Tarot. The 22 Tarot trumps are ideal for this purpose, for they correspond to the 22 Paths on the Qabalistic Tree of Life which chart man's pilgrimage via created matter to the uncreated Divine Being.

But there is no reason why we should be condemned to explore these Paths in a mental blindfold. An intelligent use of the Tarot for divination will provide us with valuable guidance in the mundane events of life and give a fair indication of likely trends in our undertakings. There is no element of fatalism in this, for no matter what course the Tarot may indicate, ultimately the choice or decision is ours.

Frank Lind admits that cartomancy (divination by cards) can be dismissed as superstition. Nevertheless he cautions: 'One must not conclude that, because so-called superstitions are more the outcome of intuition and emotions than of careful reasoning, they are therefore without the least foundation and are entirely false. Feeling exists prior to deliberative thought, the babe turns instinctively to its mother for nourishment long before its mentality has developed. Reason must always be the servant of intuition, just as science must be the handmaid of religion ...'

BRIAN H. WALLACE

CHAPTER ONE

THE MAJOR ARCANA

The twenty-two Atout or trump cards, including *The Fool* (which is rightly unnumbered), illustrate the life of a man; his joys and sorrows, hopes and despairs; friendships, enemies, marriage, illness, and final transition, either permanently to a higher sphere, or else for a while prior to reincarnation. In short, they mirror mankind in all its manifold phases.

As the Fool is the unnumbered card, it cannot logically have any position in the Major Arcana series; for order implies number, just as number does order. This card symbolizes, in its highest sense, the return of the soul to its divine source; the No-Thing, the Primal Cause or *Ayin*, of the Qabalah; that whence all manifestation emerges and into which everything must ultimately be re-absorbed.

So all earthly gain is of no account, mere folly; the road to material success leads nowhere, ends in nothing. The best position for the Fool seems to be, therefore, after the World; though this card might also be placed before the Juggler, who stands for, among

other things, the Mystery of Unity; between
that which is Above and that which is Below.

The Juggler

The Juggler (Card I) has in Italian the
name *Pagad*, that is to say 'the master of
fortune'; or the controller of his own fate.
This card represents a young man standing
behind a table, upon which are various small
articles; these are sometimes in the form of
tools like those of a cobbler, at other times
they are symbols of the four suits. The figure
has the left arm raised, with the hand
pointing heavenwards. The right hand is in
the reverse position. In the Juggler's left
hand is a wand, indicating the human Will
and the more material element; while the
pentacle, in his other hand, is the more
ethereal part of his nature. Some authorities
on the Tarot have taken the wand to
symbolize the air element, and the pentacle
to stand for that of earth; but this cannot be
the case, for the magical efficacy of the
pentacle consists in the hidden power within
it, not in its material substance.

It is through the force of Will, symbolized
by the small rod in the Juggler's hand, that
he draws down to earth the spiritual
potencies, which is why he holds the pentacle
downwards. The angle formed by his arms
makes the shape of *Aleph*. This position,
along with his wide-brimmed hat, which

resembles the sign of Eternal Life, i.e. the figure 8 lying on its side, would seem to be a primitive part of the symbolism.

Like most of the cards of the Major Arcana, this one has two aspects; one good, the other evil. From the highest point of view, the Juggler is the seeker for spiritual truth, one who employs all his powers to that end; when such powers are abused, for selfish purposes he can become a mere trickster, a cunning distorter of the truth, and in the worst sense, the servant of Satan. Sometimes the Juggler is depicted with a girdle round his waist, and a girdle was the Zoroastrian symbol of dualism.

The High Priestess
The High Priestess (Card II) is seated between two pillars, at the entrance of a Temple; these columns, similar to the arms of the Juggler, indicate positive and negative. She is passive, whereas the Juggler is active. Upon her lap is a scroll of the *Tora*, or Divine Law; she bears on her breast a solar cross (sometimes an Egyptian ansated one, such as used to be found in the hands of their deities); at her feet is a crescent moon. In some respects this symbolism would seem to be Egyptian, and the figure to be that of Isis, as she has horns on her head-dress; for the cow was held to be sacrid to Isis, and the crescent moon her Barque. But the pillars

are Boaz and Jakin, those of Solomon's Temple.

Then the first card might be taken, as 'Papus' suggests, to express Osiris in the three worlds of the Divine, Human, and Natural, and this second to signify his female companion. Here the Temple marks the delimitation between the sacred and the profane world. This Female Pope, as she is also called, is Nature in her esoteric aspect; the eternal Mysteries from the face of which the uninitiated cannot lift the veil. She is likewise the Occult Science personified. 'It is not without reason,' says Gérard van Rijnberk, 'that several occultists, and above all astrologers, have called this card: "The Gate of the Occult Sanctuary".' The scroll is only partly unrolled, is half-hidden, because it is not for all eyes to see the writing; one must first be instructed, prove oneself qualified, before one can hope to read what is on it. But this scroll is, as Jean Chaboseau remarks, really 'in one sense the Book of Thoth itself, which one opens with a finger that seems to be guided by chance, though in actuality by intuition and inspiration'.

As for the two pillars, they are the opposing forces of good and evil at the threshold of the Mysteries, and one who enters the Occult Sanctuary may tread with reverence or profane it. *Beth*, the Hebrew letter for this card, has somewhat the shape of an open mouth, and its signification is 'House'. Surely, then, one of the meanings of this card is that one must guard one's utterances, not betray that which should be kept secret.

The High Priestess, is spiritual enlightenment, inner illumination; that deep understanding of higher truths which cannot be conveyed to the outer world, by word of mouth. And as the body is the house of the soul, one has to be cautious as to what enters in and goes out of it; keep watch at the portal of one's soul, as the High Priestess does at the entrance to the Temple.

The Empress

The Empress (Card III) is also seated, upon a kind of throne; she holds, in her right hand, a sceptre; wears a crown jewelled with stars. In the foreground, at her feet, is a field of corn; lying on which, at her right side, is a shield marked with the symbol of Venus. She symbolizes generation, the universal vivifying principle, embodied in humanity and all living forms. In contrast to the High Priestess, the chaste and perpetually celibate Diana, she is the fecund mother of everything that grows. She is Gæa (the Earth) united to Uranus (lit. Heaven).

Sometimes an eagle is shown on her shield, the bird sacred to Zeus (Sanskrit, *dyaus* the bright sky); her crown with its shining orbs

The Juggler

The High Priestess

The Empress

The Emperor

is another link with the region of the upper
air. Her sceptre indicates her control over
Nature; which influence, unlike that of the
magus, is a passive one, such as is exercised
by woman in the generation of beings. She is,
in short, universal fecundity. The water
streaming between the trees in the
background is the vivifying principle of
human beings, animals, and plants – the
Water of Life. Were one to attempt to relate
this card with the previous one of 'Isis',
though here no Egyptian symbolism is
apparent, one might say that the flowing
water suggests the source of the Nile, from
which flows the force that sustains and
fructifies, after giving the outlet to Life.

Since the seed is first in darkness, as is the
child in the womb, and all emerges from
darkness into the light of day under the rays
of the sun; therefore one of the meanings of
this card is 'Darkness of Night'. One might
almost say that it refers to the marriage of
Light with Darkness. The Empress is the
'Queen of Life', and the symbol of production
through the female principle, which is one of
feeling rather than thought; it is intuitive,
emotional, more than intellectual. She is
sometimes said to represent Ishtar, the
Babylonian Goddess of Fertility, the Mother
of all; whose worship spread, from her
counterpart in Egypt, to Greece and Rome.
She was worshipped under various names in

the different countries where she was for long held in great veneration.

She was the 'Many-breasted' Artemis, and bore the titles of 'Silver-Shining', 'Seed-Producing', and 'Pregnant'. Ashtarte in Canaan, and Attar in Mesopotamia, she was also Ashtar in Moab, Athtar in Southern Arabia, Astar in Abyssinia, Atargatis in Syria, Astarte in Greece; while, as M. Esher Harding remarks in her work *Woman's Mysteries*, 'Artemis seems to be the general term used for any of the many manifestations of this great and all-powerful goddess – the Magna Dea of the East.'

This author tells us that Ishtar 'ruled successively over all the moon cycles or months of the year; and the fertility of the year, all that was born during the twelve months, was considered to be the offspring of Ishtar. This idea was beautifully expressed in the belief that her son, Tammuz, was actually in his own person the vegetation of the earth. He is called Urikittu, the Green One.' Clearly, the sceptre which the Empress holds in her right hand, as depicted on this card, emphasizes the fixation in matter of the spiritual, life-giving forces.

Acca Larentia, a goddess to whom the Romans entrusted their seed-corn and their dead (*Lares*) may also fitly be associated with this card. One then sees a connection between Card XIII, the final harvesting, and this sowing of the Spirit in the earthly soil. Otherwise the Empress is Ceres (or Demeter). The Egyptian goddess Nephthys, who represented the generative aspect of darkness, as the god Set did the destructive one, was depicted carrying an ear of corn in her hand.

The Emperor
The Emperor (Card IV) shows us a crowned figure who, in the pack of the Insight Institute cards, is seated on a throne and holding in his right hand a sceptre in the form of the Egyptian *ankh*, or sign of life. Whereas the Empress relates, in one sense, to the ruler of the hearth and the home-life, the Emperor stands for domination of the world without: kingship, government, leadership, control of the masses – in short, temporal power. The Emperor is the Regent of *this* World.

Again, here we have the active, the male principle. That which has been born in the world has to be expanded, developed, directed. There are many realms to be conquered. The rams' heads (the Ram being the emblem of Mars) intimate the martial character of the Emperor, as does also the firm pose of the figure's hands and feet. He is an old man, with a long beard, which denotes long endurance, and completion; this last being one of the meanings of the card.

Be it noted, the sceptre is the same symbol of regeneration as is seen on the shield of the Empress, but it is balanced by the ball with the cross; the cross, being above the sphere, signifies that the spiritual power is above the temporal, that the will in its progressive activity must be kept under control by the spirit. Furthermore, the sphere may be taken, from another angle, to represent the domination of the Adept over Matter; symbolized in a general sense by the Hermetic Globe, which points to control of the inferior elements.

We see symbolized in the first four cards of the Major Arcana, taken in their order: Mind, Spirit (that is, the reflex of the Divine Nature), Soul (the vehicle of feelings and emotions), and the Will. The meanings of the cards, as a whole, unfold in a logical sequence, from the Juggler (or Magus) to the Fool. Card I is the nucleus, it *must be* the starting-point, of all the others; for primarily understanding is essential to any development. 'In the beginning was the Word,' implies understanding.

The Pope
The Pope, or Hierophant (Card V) signifies, in its highest sense, spiritual rule, in

contradistinction to the more material and less lasting domination of the Emperor. Rightly, the Hierophant's kingdom is not of this earth. However, it *is* to the extent that the priest gives instruction to the people.

Broadly, the High Priestess represents the Hindu *sruti* (divine revelation), and the Pope the *smriti* (traditional teaching). He is the ruling power in external religion, his tuition is practical and oral, so he has no need of a scroll or book (intuition), as in the case of the High Priestess. His teaching is exoteric, suited to the masses, whereas hers is esoteric and can only be conveyed to the initiated. So Christ spoke in parables to the multitude, while to just a select few, His disciples, He disclosed the mysteries of the Kingdom of Heaven.

This intructor in traditional beliefs, the repository of theological dogmas, is in ecclesiastical vestments. His throne has two uprights at its back, reminding one of the pillars of the Temple between which the High Priestess is seated; he has on the pontifical crown, in his left hand he holds a triple cross, and his right one is uplifted with two fingers raised in benediction.

'The Sceptre with the triple Cross,' says H.T. Morley, 'is certainly an egyptian relic, having relation to the triple Phallus, which represents the recovery of Osiris.' We are informed likewise by 'Papus', that 'The triple

Cross represents the triple *lingam* of Indian theogony; that is to say, the penetration of the creative power throughout the Divine, the Intellectual, and the Physical Worlds, which causes all the manifestations of universal life to appear.'

The two upright posts at his back are, symbolically, one the Law and the other Liberty; this duality, which is repeated again and again in the pictorial diagrams of these cards, emphasizes that freedom of choice which we all possess, that pull in two opposite directions which is the very essence of individual existence and our progress depends uopn our response one way or the other. The figures on either side of the Hierophant are no doubt of two kinds; one a 'sheep', and the two others 'goats'.

It may be asked: 'Why has the Pope a small Maltese cross upon the back of each of the gloves which he wears?' Well, gloves are emblematic of honesty and purity, when worn by the clergy, to intimate that the servants of God have clean hands and receive no bribes, nor any gifts that may corrupt. Gérard van Rijnberk tells us that 'pontifical gloves', so referred to by Innocent III, were formerly ornamented with a little disc of gold or gilded metal, which had in its centre a simple Maltese cross.

He further informs us that 'Among the oldest of these gloves that have been

preserved is the pair once belonging to Saint
Basil of Essen Cathedral (twelfth century).'
The eight points of the Maltese cross
symbolize the eight beatitudes, and this card
therefore links Christianity with the religious
beliefs of ancient Egypt.

The Lovers

The Lovers (Card VI) very definitely lays
stress upon the choice each of us has of
taking one of two divergent paths, one to the
right and the other to the left. In certain
Tarot packs (as in that of the Insight
Institute) this arcanum shows a youthful
figure of the male sex standing between two
females, who are the embodiments of Vice
and Virtue; one wishes to lead him to take
the path to the right, the other to the left. He
hesitates as to which direction he shall take.

At other times, a couple of lovers are
pictured as being united in matrimony by a
third party. The former is almost certainly
the older symbolism. Prodicus, a sophist and
rhetorician of Cos, who lived about 396 B.C.,
has put on record in his writings how
Hercules, when he had reached manhood,
was tempted by two females,one possessing
all the attractions of Vice, the other the more
austere ones of Virtue. Finally, after some
hestitation, he yielded to the persuasions of
Virtue. We have now only the substance of
this celebrated fable of the *Choice of Hercules*;

preserved by Xenophon, in his *Memorabilia*.

At the top of this card is almost always a being with a bow, shooting an arrow at the central figure, or figures, below. Undoubtedly this item, practically the only constant one, is the key to the situation. The bow is a symbol of the Eternal Spirit, the arrow is that of Divine Impulsion: Karmic urges, one might think, must prompt the young man to take this or that path. In this sense, the archer can be taken to be, as is the view of 'Papus', the spirit of Justice floating in a radiant halo above the group. But it is not conclusive, as he suggests is the fact, that the arrow of Punishment is being aimed at the personification of Vice. Indeed, the figure at which the arrow is pointed often varies.

If one rejects this particular design; then the dual aspects of good and evil, which appear repeatedly on the cards of the Major Arcana, will in this case be lost.

The Chariot

The Chariot (Card VII) pictures a man in a chariot drawn by two horses. We see, at a glance, that the charioteer has a crown on his head, a sceptre in his right hand; so evidently the car is one of triumphal progress. In some packs this vehicle is drawn by two lions, elsewhere a couple of oxen, and in one pack at least by a black and a white lion, both having a sphinx's head. Waite says the

The Pope

The Lovers

The Chariot

The Balance

charioteer is 'the King in his triumph, typifying, however, the victory which creates kingship with its natural consequences.' From a materialistic point of view this interpretation will hold, but there is surely a much deeper signification.

Waite thinks that the charioteer is 'conquest on all planes – in the mind, in science, in progress, in certain trials of intuition'; but that the tests of initiation through which he has triumphantly passed are on a lower level, and so that 'if he came to the pillars of that Temple between which the High Priestess is seated, he could not open the scroll of the *Tora*, nor if she questioned him could he answer. He is not hereditary royalty and he is not priesthood.' But, although this card may convey the idea of the Magus who has conquered upon the lower plane, having learnt to master and direct the elementary forces for his own ends, it can have another, a secondary and more lofty signification, as 'Papus' gives one to believe; for he says that this seventh card of the Tarot represents 'Man performing the function of God the Creator.'

There are four columns supporting the canopy of the chariot. These columns are said to refer to the four elements: fire, air, water, and earth; also the four creatures of Card XXI. Each pillar is divided into two equal parts, reminding us as Foster Case says, of the hermetic maxim: 'That which is above is as that which is below.'

On either shoulder of the charioteer is a face looking in opposite directions, outwards; the horses have their heads turned inwards. The faces are supposed to be the Urim and Thummim, according to 'Papus', of the sovereign sacrificant. Once more we have the carnal and spiritual urges, which the charioteer has apparently well in hand (for the animals are moving forward in a quite docile manner), indicated on this card.

It is possible that the two horses might also symbolize the two more subtle bodies of man, over which the charioteer has control; though this notion seems rather far-fetched. Anyway, the charioteer may be regarded as the young man of the previous card, who is now moving ahead, whether to his advantage or not will depend upon the extent to which he keeps his low promptings from running away with him. Still, as the figure on this card is not guiding the horses, which are proceeding without reins, it looks as though he has completely mastered his animal passions. Which is the higher aspect of this arcanum.

The number 7 is, of course, a holy number, and plays an important part in mysticism. According to ancient teaching, Man is composed of seven properties which are under the influence of the seven planets. One may take it that the Magus has here reached the end of his first stage of development.

The Balance

The Balance (Card VIII), otherwise Justice, intimates that we must all be weighed in the balance; that each one of us is indeed receiving his or her exact due daily, according to one's merits. Here it is Divine Justice that is referred to, and so the figure on this arcanum is not blindfolded. Man-made justice must be to some extend blind, whereas Divine Justice views all things with strict impartiality. Beyond question this symbolism is extremely ancient.

The early Egyptians believed that the soul of the dead was conducted to the Judgement Hall of Osiris, there to be weighed in the 'Great Balance', in his presence, by Thoth. To Thoth was attributed the invention of letters and writing; he was the scribe of the gods, being something in the nature of the Egyptian Recording Angel. If the heart, which was placed in one pan, exactly balanced a feather (*Maat*), symbolic of righteousness, then the soul of the deceased was rewarded for its good deeds and went to dwell henceforth with the gods.

According to the Koran, everyone will be weighed, similarly, in the scales of the archangel Gabriel; one's good works being put into the scale called 'Light', and the evil

ones in the scale called 'Darkness'. Among
the Greeks, Astræa, the goddess of Equity,
was said to have lived upon earth in the
Golden Age, until sin began to prevail. She
then withdrew with the last of the gods into
the sky, being metamorphosed into the
constellation Virgo. In keeping with this
myth it would seem that Virgo must be the
astrological affinity of this card, whereas
'Papus' gives it as Cancer, and Paul Foster
Case as Libra.

The sword of Justice, we need scarcely
remark, is a double-edged one and cuts both
ways. Says 'Papus': 'Occult science (2), at
first theoretical, has become practical (5),
and has been taught verbally. Now it appears
in all the pitilessness of consequences,
terrible for the false Magi (the Sword), but
just towards the true Initiates (Balance).' In
Qabalistic terminology, the seated woman
represents *Chesed* (Mercy); the Sword,
Geburah (Severity, the Rigour of the Law);
and the Balance itself, the equilibrium
(*Tiphereth*, the centre of Harmony), kept
rightly between the two.

One may point out that the pans of the
scales form again the figure 8 upon its side,
as in the case of the Juggler's hat, being (as
we have already remarked) the symbol for
Eternal Life. The eyes, placed on either side
of the nose, are like the two pans of a balance
with the upright between them. So one might

say that the Balance intimates that we are all being watched and weighed up by the Eternal Eyes.

The Hermit

The Hermit (Card IX) is not a recluse in the true sense of the word; he is not content to sit still and meditate in a cave, but is bent on exploring the outer world. There are obstacles in his path, and he must walk with caution; if he is truly a wise man, however, he knows that all impediments will be ultimately to his advantage, and that there are 'sermons in stones'. The small flame in his lantern is the light in his soul, which, however feeble, enables him to see more clearly than he could with his two unaided eyes. If he tries to find his way solely by the faint light of his intelligence, then he is sure to go astray, to stumble, and to fail to reach his objective. Rather the light of the Supreme Spirit, which is ever present however dark one's immediate surroundings, must be his constant guide.

He is no longer the Juggler performing wonderful feats of magic, nor is he the ecclesiastic (Pope) busy with religious dogmas. Instead, he is led by the illumination from the Divine, in his soul; aided by his own understanding. But if he has rightly learnt his lesson, at this stage of his development, he also lets his light shine forth to glorify his Father which is in Heaven.

However, the Hermit must be careful in doing this, and he may be too wary; for there are those who will try to extinguish the light he has gained of spiritual realities, to place further obstacles in his way, and to turn him from the path of righteousness. This might be the priest of orthodox religion, the occultist of a lower order, or the pure materialist. Having obtained the balance between things material and things spiritual, the harmony between his lower and higher impulses, he has to keep straight on, realizing that he has yet far to go before he reaches the end of his journey upon this plane of existence.

We see in the Hermit the beardless young man of Card 6, who has chosen the right path, and has obtained something of the wisdom of the aged. As 'Papus' expresses it: 'The arrow shot by the genius in the sixth arcanum has become his support, and the effulgent aureole which surrounded the genius is now imprisoned in the lamp which guides the Initiate. This is the result of prolonged effort.' His staff is that of his faith in the Supreme Being. 'I will fear no evil; for thou art with me; thy rod and thy staff they comfort me' (Psalm XXIII, 4).

The mantle is his protection from the chill winds of adverse criticism and those material doubts which may assail him. It may also be the cloak with which the Adept conceals his profound knowledge of higher truths from the eyes of the profane. Gautama Buddha said: 'The light of truth's high noon is not for tender leaves.' His lantern, furthermore, can symbolize the spark of Divinity, the unquenchable Light of the Spirit, imprisoned in the chaos of Matter. Eliphas Levi, allowing his imagination to have full play, affirms that the mantle of the Hermit is that of Apollonius of Tyana, his staff that of the pastors and patriarchs, and his lantern the lamp of Hermes Trismegistus.

The Wheel of Fortune

The Wheel of Fortune (Card X) has been referred to that of Ixion, the circle of the Zodiac, and the restless round of man's innumerable lives; the ups-and-downs of earthly existence, resulting from the working out of Karmic consequences. The same thread of ideas runs throughout. Only the creatures on the Wheel – one at each side of its rim, and a third perched upon its summit – change their form in different Tarot sets.

At the top of the Wheel, on the Insight Institute card, is Osiris, the great Egyptian divinity, regarded as the preserver of life both in this world and the next; the hue of his body is therefore rightly green, whilst the ever-green tamarisk is his sacred tree. Sometimes Osiris is replaced on this card by the Sphinx, symbolizing the eternal riddle of Creation; also the figure on top of the Wheel may be taken to be the Liberator of the soul from its round of repeated incarnations.

Upon the left side of the Wheel (facing one), and mounting towards the being at the top, is Hermanubis (Hermes-Anubis) the jackal-headed god, who watched over and conducted to judgement spirits upon their leaving earth. Anubis, it was thought, was perpetually fighting against Typhon, who is being thrown from the rim on the other side of the Wheel. Typhon (or Set) is the evil genius of Egyptian mythology. He is the equivalent of the Scandinavian Loki, also of Lucifer or Satan. On some cards he has a trident in his hand; it is pointing downwards, towards the Ocean of Samsara – the Sea of Worldliness. Typhon causes storms both at sea and in the human soul. As the Egyptians reckoned him to be responsible for all the evil in the world, they represented him as a wolf.

Everything in the cosmos is revolving, as it were, like a wheel: the stars in their courses, the seasons of the year, and the change from day to night and night to day. The celestial sphere was regarded by astronomers of old as turning round and round ceaselessly, as though upon a disc. It is interesting to note, in this connection, that St Donatus bears a wheel set round with lights. Moreover, St Euphemia and St Willigis both carry wheels.

Needless to say, it is only in a more limited way that this card signifies the ups-and-downs of fortune. Though it is a reminder, and a warning, that those who are lifted high in this world today, looking down upon others, may suddenly descend, by the spinning of the Wheel by the hand of Fate. 'For whosoever exalteth himself shall be abased; and he that humbleth himself shall be exalted' (Luke XIV, II).

The deeper meaning is that in a succession of lives, as is symbolized by the Labours of Hercules, one has to win liberation from the wearying round of reincarnation, attaining at long last the perfect equilibrium signified by Osiris, the figure poised between Good and Evil, at the top of the Wheel. This is the higher aspect of the young man of Card VI. He has now stepped out of the Chariot (Card VII) of victories upon this plane of existence, and is crowned with the laurels of a spiritual triumph. Lastly, the Wheel of Fortune may be likened to the spinning-wheel of Lachesis, which ceases to turn but for a while, when Atropos, the eldest of the Parcæ, cuts the thread of human life here on earth.

The symbolism on this card is certainly very ancient. Herodotus records how Croesus the Lydian remarked to Cyrus: 'Now if you deem yourself and the army that you lead to be immortal, it is not for me to give you advice; but if you know that you and

those whom you rule are but men, then I
must first teach you this: men's fortunes are
on a wheel, which in its turning suffers not
the same man to prosper for ever.' and by
way of pointing out how fickle is fate,
Plutarch comments, in his *Moralia, De Facie
in Orbe Lunae*, that 'In triumphs, people have
dropped down dead.' Browning similarly
gives warning, 'The high man, with a great
thing to pursue, dies ere he knows it.' In
short, it is the last turn of the Wheel which
counts most.

Upon the 'Smaragdine Tablet', or the
Emerald Tablet, were inscribed in
Phoenician characters thirteen sentences.
One of these runs: 'Ascend with the greatest
sagacity from the earth to heaven, and then
again descend to the earth, and unite
together the powers of things superior of the
whole world, and all obscurity will fly away
from you.' In other words, the Pagad must
become 'controller of his own fate', freed
from the Wheel of Fortune. In ancient Egypt,
wheels were kept revolving in the temples as
a reminder of how changeful and brief is
human existence; so records Plutarch, in his
life of Numa Pompilius.

The Enchantress

The Enchantress (Card XI) depicts a young
woman gripping a lion by its jaws. She does
not seem to be in any fear of the beast, and is

not exerting any apparent physical strength. Obviously the reaon is that she is employing spiritual courage and the power that comes from it, rather than that of the will and body.

She is the female equivalent of St George and the Dragon. The dragon as well as the lion being the symbol of the carnal urges. It will be remembered that the first labour of Hercules was the slaying of the Nemean lion. There have been many dragon-slayers: St Michael, St Margaret, St Philip, St Martha, and St Florent, all slew dragons. How old this symbolism is can be seen from the fact that as early as 312 B.C. a ceremony was performed in Egypt, in the temple of Amen-Ra at Thebes, of the spearing of Apep (the fiend of darkness, a monster who lay in wait to swallow the Sun-god). That the woman pictured on this card is wearing the same type of hat as the Juggler, its brim having the shape of the figure 8 lying on its side, is an intimation that she is exerting spiritual force.

She does not resort to any magic, such as might be used by the Juggler; but, as 'Papus' remarks, is 'the image of the sacred science (second arcanum) when justly applied (8).' Hers is the moral force of innocence, which can tame the lower passions in that of others; also she has conquered the primitive instincts in herself, and so she is fearless of (Satan) the roaring lion.

'Papus' gives Mars as the astronomical

The Hermit

The Wheel of Fortune

The Enchantress

The Hanged Man

affinity of this card. Paul Foster Case gives
Leo. Other authorities have given the Ram
or the Sun. Which shows the futility of
attempting to make the Tarot conform
strictly to the Zodiac. It seems more logical
to assume that the female is Virgo, subduing
the fiery passions of Leo, and bringing the
two sides of her nature (the two opposing
principles so often indicated in these cards)
into perfect harmony in Libra (the Balance),
the third Sun-sign of the series; in which
Virgo (Astræa) is, as it were, raised up in the
heavens, exalted.

The Hanged Man

The Hanged Man (Card XII) is a curious
representation in the respect that the figure is
suspended by the left foot and is upside-
down. He appears to be quite at ease in this
strange situation and is as placid as the
Enchantress. His right leg is crossed behind
the left, and the side posts of the gibbet have
each six lopped branches along their length.

The man's crossed legs form roughly a
cross indicating the cardinal points of the
compass, while the lopped branches refer to
the completion of the cycle of the Sun
through the twelve Signs of the Zodiac. Also
the implication is that the Labours of
Hercules are at an end. The man may still be
to some extent earth-bound, but he has
attained at least a measure of perfection and

is all but released from the rim of the turning Wheel, the sufferings and illusions imposed by repeated embodiments in the flesh.

If he has not yet reached Nirvana (the final deliverance of his soul from bondage to earth), he is now at least partially free, the balance has swung in the right direction and only the astral link (the thong by which he is attached to matter) has to be broken.

In its highest sense this card signifies voluntary sacrifice. As the man has his eyes turned towards the sky, we may conclude that they are now opened to celestial things; sometimes coins are shown falling from his pockets, an indication that he has abandoned all claims to the riches of this world. However, there are other interpretations. One is that the upside-down position of the figure symbolizes the incarnation of spirit in Matter (the inverted reflection, as it were, of the Divine); also, along with the money dropping to earth, the vivification of Nature by an exterior, spiritual agency.

Jean Chaboseau quotes an authority, Maxwell, who identifies the Hanged Man with Atys (a secondary Syrio-Hellenic divinity), symbolizing the course of the sun in relation to the seasons. Atys free is then the summer solstice; bound, and hanging head downwards, the winter one.

While the right leg of the Hanged Man, bent behind the left, forms a cross; his arms folded behind his back, together with his head, form a triangle with the point downwards. The cross indicates suffering (which is here self-imposed); and the triangle (the divine spirit in man), like the pentacle in the Juggler's right hand, intervenes between his physical body and earth.

Lamed, which is the letter of the Hebrew alphabet usually assigned to this card, has roughly the shape of the Hanged Man. But, as Grillot de Givry justly remarks, the agreement between the letters of the Hebrew alphabet and the designs of the Major Arcana does not go far; and so I have not given a Hebrew letter for every one of the cards.

One may also recognize in the Hanged Man, Odin on the gallows-tree, Havamal; upon which, like Jesus, he was crucified — offered up unto himself.

The Reaper

The Reaper (Card XIII) is a gruesome design; it is of a hideous skeleton cutting with a scythe, and at the figure's feet are scattered dismembered heads and hands, and a foot. Death's scythe makes no distinctions, it is no respecter of persons. It takes toll of kings and peasants, the rich and the poor, the wise man and the fool, the saint and the sinner. Remorselessly it cuts through the worm and the wings of the butterfly alike. In its wide and mighty sweep it encompasses the whole earth.

But it must not be thought that the Reaper here refers particularly to physical death. The meaning of this arcanum penetrates far deeper than that. The grass is green with promise; the eyes in the severed heads are wide open, the hands are uplifted as if reaching for something on high, and the foot is firmly planted. What is depicted here is the death of the old self, the sloughing of all fleshly desires.

Man has, at this stage come to the realization that all material manifestations are *Maya* (Illusion); he sees himself, in the physical sense, as a mere skeleton of his real Self, which has its true abode in a higher realm. There can be no spiritual advancement for him until he has discarded the limitations and encumbrances of the flesh, metaphorically speaking, and risen from the grave of his old earthly attachments. He must be born again, of the Spirit.

He who does not face death in this sense is truly dead; but he who realizes that death must be conquered, by the regeneration of the soul, is on the way to obtaining eternal life. The sting of Death is in the soul of the unrighteous. One must not allow one's head, hands, and feet to gain the mastery over one's soul; they are to be 'cut off' in that respect. Which is what Christ meant when he said: 'If thy hand offend thee, cut if off and cast it from thee'; and 'If thine eye offend thee, pluck it out and cast it from thee.' Not in a literal sense, but by non-attachment to the physical; spiritually, an alchemical process of the transmutation of the baser metal into gold.

'Papus' says: 'The works of the head (conception) become immortal as soon as they are realized (hands and feet).' The skeleton, as the framework of the body, is, furthermore, symbolic of the union between it and the soul. When the physical body is discarded there is no need for this go-between; for the soul has then been united, upon a higher level of existence, with the Supreme Spirit. Death is the twin brother of Life; the Siva (destroyer) and Brahma (creator) of the Hindus. Creation necessitates its opposite, destruction; as the Spirit descends into dead Matter, so it must return to its source – which is Life escaping from earth, under the dark cloak of Death. Understood rightly, then, death is the link between the visible and invisible worlds; it is the Universal Transforming Principle.

The Angel of Time

The 'Angel of Time', or Temperance (Card XIV) is far more pleasing to the eye than the previous card. A winged female figure is pouring a stream of liquid, without spilling a

drop, from one vase into another. Here we
have represented the flowing of the past,
through the present, into the future. But the
wings of the Angel, and the fact that one vase
is held some distance above and widely apart
from the other, is suggestive.

This symbolism doubtless refers also to the
descent of Spirit into Matter; and, in an
individual application, the purifying of the
soul by a spiritual transfusion. St Paul says:
'There are vessels of gold and of silver, but
also of wood and of earth; and some to
honour and some to dishonour.' These four
vessels may be likened to man's four bodies,
respectively: the spiritual, astral, etheric, and
physical. The spirit must flow down into and
purify the astral.

Perhaps to emphasize this signification, in
some Tarot packs one of the vases on this
card is gold and the other silver. Again, the
astral body is eventually disposed of and the
fluid of Life flows back into the Spirit whence
it came. Among the ancient Greeks, it may
be mentioned, the pouring of the contents of
one vessel into another was held to imply
metempsychosis. H.T. Morley thinks that
the allusion may be to the pouring out of
wine or oil in an oblation to the gods, which
was one of the earliest methods employed in
consulting them, and is said to have been
used by the Babylonians at least 2,000 B.C.

Since this card follows immediately after

The Reaper

The Angel of Time

The Black Magician

The Lightning-struck Tower

the Reaper, which symbolizes the death of the old self and spiritual regeneration, we might compare this pouring of fluid from one vase into another to a cleansing of the soul, as with baptismal water.

In a broad sense, the liquid flowing from one cup to the other is the combination of active and passive forces. It is the union of the male and female principles. Spirit entering into Matter, and the reaction of Spirit upon Matter. Also the stream may be thought of as mind-stuff. When the current of one's thoughts is rightly directed, then one acts temperately; otherwise there is opposition between the higher promptings and the lower impulses. Here we have inspiration flowing down from above, the Angel then being Paul Brunton's 'Overself'; but, in a less lofty sense, the fluid is the interaction of mind upon mind, transference of thought, the influence exerted by suggestion; and even, possibly, the *Od* of Reichenbach, along with the mysterious force of Mesmer. Lastly, it is the vital fluid given out by the spiritual healer.

The Black Magician

The Black Magician (Card XV) is the exact reverse of the Magus (Juggler), when the latter is employing all his potentialities rightly. Man has fallen from Light, and is as dust upon the earth! None the less, he has been created in God's image. So soon as man begins to realize that he is like unto the Angel of Card XIV, pride enters his soul; he is tempted to use his knowledge, to exercise his occult powers, for evil purposes. Then truly he 'falls from Light' into utter Darkness; as did Lucifer, like a shining meteor dropping from heaven to earth. But Lucifer is also the light-bringer.

Lacking all knowledge of Evil, we should be as inanimate matter, having no apprehension or comprehension of Good. Therefore we must not consider this card as having solely a bad signification: the deliberate choosing of the wrong path; black magic, blind force, hatred. For out of evil may come good; there can be no progress without error, and so even the Devil has his purpose in the scheme of things. Each of us has to learn wisdom by our sins, mistakes, and consequent suffering; as Browning says: 'We fall to rise, are baffled to fight better, sleep to wake.'

Upon this Tarot card the Devil is standing on a small circular pedestal, a sort of mock throne. His hands are held in the opposite position from those of the Juggler; the left one is lowered, the right held up as if reversing the Pope's gesture of benediction. He holds in his left hand a flaming torch; has ribbed wings similar to those of a bat, claw-like feet, and on either side of his cap jut out jagged horns. The Devil is of both sexes; roped to his pedestal; one on either side, are two little creatures, male and female, these being the carnal urges.

The central figure of this card is that of Pan, the god of Nature; the cause of man's instinctive behaviour, of his blind follies. In some Tarot sets the Devil is represented with the extremities of a goat; the he-goat being a prototype of Satan. The appearance of Satan as a goat was usual at the witches' Sabbat.

This Goat of Mendes, a combination of faun, satyr, and Pan-goat, became in medieval times a definite synthesis of the anti-divinity. At Mendes, a city of ancient Egypt, Pan under this form was worshipped with the greatest solemnity.

The flaming candle or torch in the Black Magician's hand is agitated by the gusts of uncontrolled passions that disturb the peace of the soul in its moments of temptation and doubt. However, this burning brand is also the purifying flame of the conscience; it destroys all that is decaying, the foul and putrid matter within the soul, preparing the soil for a new and stronger growth of righteousness.

Here the Angel's wings have been transformed into those of the Devil. His torch has been thought by some to be, furthermore, a phallic symbol. Those who would penetrate into the occult mysteries must employ the critical faculty of the High Priestess, the wisdom and caution of the Hermit, or they may burn their fingers in the flame of the Devil's torch.

Paul Foster Case says of the two smaller figures, the *Panisci* or attendant imps of the central one, that they stand for 'self-conscious and subconscious modes of human mentality.' They might more reasonably be assumed to be, one an *eudaimon* (good spirit), and the other a *kakodaimon* (bad spirit). Though I think they really symbolize the male and female promptings towards virtue or vice, which we all possess; for each of us is, to a greater or lesser extent, something of the opposite sex. Dr George Divine, in his treatise *The Psychology of Everyman*, puts forward the theory that 'not only is the Personality composed of two distinct units, but that these two component units psychologically speaking are sex-differentiated.' For a proper balance to exist, the predominant personality must be kept in check by that of the opposite sex, by the 'dormant personality-unit'.

The Lightning-struck Tower

The Lightning-struck Tower, called also *The House of God* (Card XVI), is in some respects an ominous card. When man sells his soul to the Devil, uses his occult knowledge for evil ends, as does the Black Magician; then destruction descends upon him from Heaven. 'Be not deceived; God is not mocked: for whatsoever a man sows, that shall he also reap' (Galatians VI: 7).

This Atout has in its centre a tower which is struck, so it seems, by lightning in a clear sky; or, as we should say, by a 'bolt from the blue'. Two men are being hurled to earth from the tower's riven summit. Their fortress has been invaded, they have fallen from their material security. One of the figures is crowned, and has been the first, so it appears, to fall from his high estate, while the other is dressed like a rustic.

Divine Justice, like the scythe of the Reaper, takes no count of social inequalities. He who is a tower of strength unto himself, blind to his own weakness, may suddenly find his illusions shattered. Upon some cards, as in the pack of the Insight Institute, the sun is shining down upon the Tower, instead of its being struck by lightning. This conveys the higher meaning of the cards, that the darkness of the soul is suddenly illumined by a flood of light from above, a Divine fulguration.

Then the Tower may be likened to man's physical body, in which he is kept imprisoned by the bricks and mortar of his fleshly tenement, his carnal limitations. How narrow is his outlook is emphasized by the three small windows of the Tower, symbolizing no doubt the restricted outlook of his body, soul, and spirit; from which he can only catch a glimpse of Heaven in the darkness with which he has surrounded himself of his own choice.

A time arrives, however, when an illumining flash from on high sets him free; the darkness is dispelled; he is released from his self-imposed captivity. His past little world of inner satisfaction is destroyed; he must build for himself a new dwelling upon a sounder foundation. His body has now to become the House of God. A woman is sometimes pictured on this card; she is weeping outside the destroyed tower. She is Mother Nature, witnessing the destruction of her material edifice; this is the revolt of the flesh robbed of its prisoner.

This card can also refer, in the case of an advanced soul, to complete liberation from the bondage of the flesh. The soul has no further need to be embodied; it has won its release from the tirelessly turning Wheel (Card X) of Reincarnation. it will be noted that, on the Insight Institute card, little golden drops are being scattered on either side at the top of the Tower. These are shown on some cards as pointed flames.

Upon cards of the Marseilles Tarot type they are represented as tiny jets of flame, pointing upwards in the case of the Sun and

downwards in that of the Moon. On Card
XVIII (the Moon) of the Tarot of Français
Jerger (seventeenth century) they are all
directed towards earth, and on Card XIX
towards the centre of the Sun. These balls or
jets of fire symbolize all that descends from
above or ascends on high. That which is
spiritual with regard to the Sun, and astral in
respect of the Moon. When illumination
comes, one's eyes are opened to what comes
from on high; the Manna falling from
Heaven, more enriching than the golden
coins of an earthly Mint which fall from the
Hanged Man's pockets.

The Star

The Star (Card XVII) is the Star of Hope. It
is the promise of a new and brighter dawn. In
the Koran we are told of the stars: 'They
serve also as a guard against every rebellious
Satan.' This card balances the evil effects of
the preceding one. Here we have a clear
intimation that the fall is not irreparable.
The eternal spark cannot be extinguished.
Again it is said in the Koran, of Abraham:
'And when the night overshadowed him, he
beheld a star.'

It is because of our inner knowledge that
we are but 'broken lights' of God, we have
the assurance that He will not finally forsake
us; thus it is that 'Hope springs eternal in the

human breast.' The Magi followed a star, and it may be said that all truly wise men follow *one* star.

Pictured upon this card is a young woman kneeling by a river; she has, like the figure on card XIV, two vases in her hands; but now she is emptying the contents of both of them upon the ground. The liquid pouring from the vessels is the spiritual and astral fluids, which have at this stage been widely diffused, have soaked as it were into the earth.

Near the woman is sometimes pictured an ibis (or else a butterfly upon a flower). The ibis was the symbol of the soul in ancient Egypt, and the chief enemy of the serpent; it appears at the rise of the Nile, but disappears at its inundation. For the Greeks, of course, the butterfly symbolized the soul. Above the kneeling figure are seven stars; an eighth, larger than the others, is just over her head, at the top of the card. Astrologically, these smaller stars are the Pleiades; according to mythology, the seven daughters of Atlas. After death they are placed in the heavens, where they formed a constellation called Pleiades, near the back of the Bull in the Zodiac. They all, with the exception of Merope, who married Sisyphus, king of Corinth, had immortal gods for their suitors. One of the stars, it will be observed, on the Insight Institute card, is paler than the rest; that is because Merope hid herself out of

shame at her marriage with a mortal,
therefore her star is dim and obscured.

Be it noted that in each of these five-
pointed stars the pentacle points upward;
which is the case with the good pentagram,
whereas the evil one points downward. The
eighth star, perhaps, emphasizes that these
stars are of one group, and that Maia is the
most luminous. Sometimes the Black
Magician is shown with an inverted
pentagram upon his forehead.

Man is said to have a septenary nature, to
be composed of seven principles; in the
terminology of Theosophy, he possesses
Rupa, or *Sthula-Sarira* (the physical body),
Prana (vital principle), *Linga Sarira* (astral or
phantom double), *Manas* (dual principle of
Mind; the higher and lower intelligence),
Buddhi (the Spiritual Soul), and *Atman*
(Spirit, One with the Absolute). Shakespeare
discourses upon the seven ages of man. The
normal span of a man's life is three score
years and ten.

There are Seven Bodies in Alchemy: Sun
for gold, Moon for silver, Mars iron,
Mercury quicksilver, Saturn lead, Jupiter
tin, and Venus copper. The young woman on
this card may be identified with Hebe, the
Goddess of Youth, who was cup-bearer to the
gods and supplied them with nectar. She had
the power of restoring the aged to the full
vigour of youth. Hermetically, the fluid she

pours from the vases is that of Amrita, the
ambrosia of the Hindu gods; the Draught of
Immortality, the Elixir of Life.

In one sense, the large star over the figure's
head is the Egyptian *Sahu*, glorified body,
which is born with man – it is the 'Body of
Fire, or Star' – that enters heaven and lives
with Osiris and the blessed for all eternity.
'Oh, never star was lost but it rose afar!'

The Moon

The Moon (Card XVIII) is most interesting.
It is divided into three planes: the lower
astral, the mental, and the celestial regions;
the emotional, mental, and spiritual levels.
These three planes symbolize the tripartite
composition of the soul, the two lower levels
being the down-curve of the Hindu Wheel of
Samsara. Philo Judaeus described three
states in the manifested universe as here
depicted.

In the lowest section of this card, a crayfish
(Cancer, the zodiacal sign of the Crab, is
ruled by the Moon) is seen crawling out of
the water on to dry land. Man's mind is
fluidic until it rises from the purely
instinctive to a firmer and more stable level.
This part of the card indicates all that is
veiled in the twilight of the subconscious;
influenced by the light of the Moon, which is
a borrowed and false one, distorting
everything.

Here we see suggested, also the evolution of species; the development of man from an amphibious, anthropodous creature, into a human being who walks upright. 'Doth not man perceive that we have created him of the moist germs of life?' questions the Koran. 'Yet, lo! is he an open caviller.' A secondary implication is that the subconscious, if one is not on one's guard, may invade the territory of the waking consciousness and so perturb the mind with many creeping fears and crawling horrors.

Two dogs occupy the centre of the middle section of this card. They are howling up at the Moon pictured at the top of it; or rather *the old moon in the new moon's arms*, illustrating the Moon's various phases. These dogs are a reference to Hecate, who was in Greek mythology the goddess of the dark moon; she was represented with three heads, one being that of a dog. She was always accompanied by baying hounds. As her power extended over not only the earth, but the sea, hell and heaven, she links up with all three sections of the card.

One of the dogs is in some packs replaced by a wolf. To the right and left of the animals are two towers. These mark the limits of the material world, in contradistinction to the infinite expanse of the celestial one. 'Papus' says that this card symbolizes the stage at which the spirit has become completely

materialized. 'The entry of Spirit into Matter
is so great a fall that everything conspires to
augment it. Servile spirits (the dog), savage
souls (the wolf), and crawling creatures (the
crayfish), are all present watching the fall of
the soul, hoping to aid in its destruction.'

Between the two dogs, on the Insight
Institute card, is an unrolled scroll,
reminding us of that of the High Priestess;
upon it is printed MA, with a couple of
strokes on either side. It has been argued that
the symbolism of this card, if not the card
itself, is Atlantean; since the submerged
continent was called Ma or Mu, and two
oblique strokes in Ma's hieratic alphabet
stand for 'land'.

Unfortunately for this view, the strokes on
the card do not appear to be oblique but are
upright. However, in support of the theory,
one may mention that before the deluge the
continent was split by strife. But Ma would
more likely refer to Lemuria, the land of our
lunar ancestors; for *Maha* means 'great', and
the Lemurians are said to have had immense
astral bodies. Furthermore, Ma is the root of
Maya (Illusion). Which later is the worst
aspect of this card. Would one read the *Tora*
rightly, the writing on the scroll of the High
Priestess, one must do so by the light of the
Sun; not that of the Moon.

Goethe has summed up the meaning of
this card, without any intentional reference

to the Tarot in his *Faust: 'Ales vergangliche ist nur ein Gleichnis'* (Everything in our transitory world is but a resemblance.)

Against the claim that the symbolism of this card dates back to Atlantean times, which seems highly improbable, one may mention that Herodotus states, though one wonders upon what authority, that the Atlanteans did not dream. This card, however, certainly refers primarily to the dream world, which is that of the working of the subconscious mind.

An interesting point worth noting in connection with the card is that on it are shown, in some Tarot packs, tiny jets of ascending flame. These are spirits of the departed hovering between earth and the Moon, to which they were believed to pass before returning earthward for reincarnation, or else passing on to the Sun. It is said that one of the chief causes of the Boxer Rising was that the Chinese superstitiously believed that the spires of churches built by Christian missionaries interfered with the free movement of spirits in the upper air.

But there is a higher interpretation of the symbolism of this card. *Ma* is also the root of the word Mary, and the association of the Holy Virgin with the moon is clearly expressed in the writings of the Catholic Fathers. In the loftiest sense the Moon is the

The Star

The Moon

The Sun

The Day of Judgement

female preservative principle exalted in the heavens, the Moon Mother watching over the birth of the Christ child, of the spirit entering into the material world, and preventing its light from extinction.

The Sun

The Sun (Card **XIX**) now shines forth in its full brilliance. After the moontide of its despair, the soul emerges into the light of a brighter day. Man must awaken to the realization of how great is the darkness encompassing him, feel how near he is to blindness, before he can look with new eyes upon the world. It is always darkest just before the dawn.

Upon the Insight Institute card, a naked child is seen riding on a white horse, in the blazing light of the sun; lifted on high, in the child's left hand, is an unfurled banner. The horse symbolizes the purified soul, stressed further by the naked child stripped of all outer pretences; while the banner betokens freedom from all material bonds.

Though the wall indicates that the soul is still in the visible world, it is no longer guided by a reflected light, as in the preceding arcanum, but by the rays of the Golden Lamp of Heaven, the giver and sustainer of life upon this planet, the outward manifestation of the divine source of its being.

On the other side of the wall are to be seen the heads of sunflowers. As the sunflower always turns its face towards the sun, so must the soul of man ever look upward to the celestial Giver of Light. When the Hermit has attained to the wisdom of a little child, he can cast aside his lantern; he will need but one lamp to show him the proper path through life, the Sun of righteousness which arises 'with healing in his wings' and dispels all darkness.

This card illustrates quite clearly a spiritual victory over the lower nature, the Divine Light shining from on high into the regenerated soul. This is a very different triumph from that of the charioteer of Card VII, which is conquest upon a more material plane. We see now the banner of Spiritual Freedom unfurled, the soul no longer restricted by any earthly ambitions. It rides forth in the world, not proceeding on foot and cloaked with caution like the Hermit, but shameless in its new-born innocence, hiding nothing from the outer world and conscious solely of its search for Truth.

Eliphas Levi says that the representation of a child on a white horse and displaying a banner is much better than the alternative one, which sometimes replaces it, of a spinner unwinding Destinies. Sometimes this card pictures two children, naked, or almost so, facing water and running hand in hand.

The Day of Judgement

The Day of Judgement (Card **XX**) obviously illustrates a purely Hebraic conception. Three figures are seen rising from the grave; the central one of the male sex, the others being female. They are, presumably, a man with his wife and daughter. Emerging from a luminous cloud above their heads is an angel, blowing a trumpet decorated with a small square flag, having on it a cross with limbs of equal length.

As the figures are of indeterminate age, none of them very old or very young, one may conclude that the intimation is that the soul is ageless; also, since we come naked into this world and leave it naked, they are unclothed. We shall be judged neither by our outward appearance nor the length of our years, but according to our works. There is a halo around the angel's head and a blaze of light about the cloud out of which the trumpeter leans. Upon the day of Resurrection, says the Koran, 'when there shall be a blast on the trumpet and ye shall come in crowds', then 'the sun and the moon shall be together.'

Actually, the Day of Judgement is no final, universal event, fixed at some definite point in time. It may come at any moment, for each one of us. We can rise from the grave of our old dead self now, while we are still in the physical body, if our ears are not deaf to the trumpet call from on high.

What is the signification, though, of the small cross upon the flag attached to the trumpet? Probably it is a solar symbol. Its shape is that of the gammadion, the fylfot (the Buddhist cross) with its terminations cut off. This would signal the cessation of the turning of the Wheel (Card X), the restlesss round of countless reincarnations; by the arresting finger of Karma, the soul having reached the state of Nirvana, the end of its long earthly pilgrimage, though this part of the symbolism is not, then, Hebraic.

Nirvana does not mean, as is often wrongly supposed, the complete extinction of the personality; it is the reaping of the ripe ear of corn, the binding of the single stalk together with others in a golden sheaf, to be gathered up in the arms of the Eternal Harvester. The bread that came down from heaven, of which he that eateth 'shall live for ever', returns to heaven. This card is essentially that of eternal life.

As Card II refers to the 'closed mouth', or one which does not give utterance to the Divine Mysteries, so Card XI is that of 'controlled speech' and the silencing of the voice of the tempter; while this card, XX, indicates that upon the Day of Judgment all secrets will be revealed. At the burial of the dead in ancient Egypt was performed the ceremony of the Opening of the Mouth, the mummy's mouth being touched with the *Ur-heka*; so that the resurrected soul might be able to answer for its past acts when questioned by the Two and Forty Assessors of the Dead.

The World
The World (Card **XXI**) illustrates the ecstatic state of the soul when it has become fully conscious of its divine origin; when the scales have fallen from man's eyes, he sees the world with a new vision, that 'Earth's crammed with heaven, and every common bush afire with God.' No longer is his soul (Psyche) like a butterfly, 'but a caterpillar dressed'; he stands naked before his Maker, rejoicing in the Divine Light within and about him. His whole being dances in its new-born freedom, sings with the morning stars. He hears the music of Orpheus, ten thousand harps that tune angelic harmonies; is in harmony with the spheres.

This card shows a female figure, quite naked save for a ribbon falling across the lower part of her person, surrounded by an elliptical laurel wreath. In either hand she holds a short wand. These rods are the positive and negative, the centrifugal and centripetal forces of Nature; they symbolize the Solar and Lunar attractions. At the corners of the garland, which has four opened flowers marking the cardinal points of the compass, are symbols of the four elements.

Of these symbols one is that of an ox, representing earth; a lion for fire; an eagle for air; and a man, or angel, for water. There is, however, some difference of opinion as to which are the correct elements to be assigned to the last two. Some authorities think, in contradiction to my view, that the eagle stands for water, and the man (or angel) for air. These four figures, which it has been stated were borrowed by St John from Ezekiel, who copied them from Assyria and Babylon, are further said to represent the four seasons, the four mysterious letters of the *Tora*, the four principal metals, and much besides. Certainly they indicate the four suits of the Minor Arcana.

Another interpretation of this card is that it symbolizes the Macrocosm or Universe, of which man is the Microcosm; the 'little world' or epitome. This is a logical conclusion. For man is, in a sense, a minute solar system.

Take note that the woman has her left leg crossed behind the right one, in contradistinction to the Hanged Man, who has his right leg crossed behind the left. This would seem to imply that, after self-sacrifice, the soul has gained its reward; once more it stands upright, as it were, lord of all it

surveys. When Spirit ceases to cling to
Matter, then it gains mastery over it; comes
to the realization that ultimately Spirit and
Matter are one. But the woman's right foot is
upon the earth, which shows that the soul
has obtained control over the material world,
which is Spirit in its lower aspect.

The Fool

The Fool (the unnumbered card of the Major
Arcana) is at once the most perplexing and
profound of all the Atouts. Whereas the
Juggler has one hand pointing towards
heaven and the other towards earth, that is to
say he is of both worlds, looks above and
below, the Fool goes his way regardless of all
earthly objects around him; he has flung to
the winds all caution, the wordly prudence of
the Hermit, he is blind to everything but the
City Beautiful of his ideal quest. In the
highest sense he is the mystic, the dreamer,
the beholder of visions.

What matters the dog at his heels, he
cannot stay to turn back in his march foward
to his distant goal; he must not be retarded
by any trivial passing events, all his thoughts
are concentrated upon his high aim. The
small things of this earth are of no account to
him for whom the Kingdom of Heaven is
already at hand. He has come to realize that
all of this changing world is *Maya* (Illusion),
that man, however wise he may be judged to

The World   *The Fool*

be by an earthly standard, is in reality a Fool. He who thinks he walks with wisdom, truly has folly for a companion.

Upon this card is depicted a man in parti-coloured clothes, who is walking towards what is seemingly a precipice, quite unaware of the danger; for his head is turned aside, and his attention directed elsewhere. Slung over his right shoulder, he carries a small bundle on a stick. The bundle contains not only all his worldly possessions, of which he needs but few, but it may be taken to be the sum-total of all his past experiences, which in his estimation really amount to nothing. Though the knowledge he has gained is small enough, it is all that he can take with him into the next world; or his future incarnation.

His memories are behind him, his hopes lie in a wide vista before him.

Still, he is perhaps unwise in not heeding the dog. One may be gazing up at heaven for what is just at one's feet. Dog spelt backwards is God. On the other hand, a so-called fool may in his darkness stumble upon what wise men, like the Hermit, have long hunted for by the light of a lantern, in vain.

A crocodile is also sometimes to be seen at the Fool's feet, upon this card. The crocodile was a symbol of deity among the Egyptians, because it is the only animal, says Plutarch, which has its eyes covered with a thin transparent membrane, so that it can see though it may not be seen; thus God sees all, without himself being seen.

The Thebans deemed crocodiles to be most sacred. One of these animals, trained to be quite tame, was kept and carefully guarded by them in every locality; it was decorated with ornaments of glass and gold, bracelets being put on its forefeet. Special food was provided for the creature, also propitiatory offerings were made to it; the best possible treatment was given it until its death, when it was embalmed and buried in a coffin.

A charming little episode in that great Indian epic the *Mahabharata* tells how Yudhishthira upon reaching the gate of heaven was refused entry because he had his dog with him. Yudhishthira decided to remain with his dog outside. However, as love and virtue cannot be kept out of heaven, he and his dumb companion were allowed to enter after all. Then the dog changed shape, became transformed into none other than the god of justice himself. Which demonstrates that we can be, at any moment, 'entertaining angels unawares' – and even, it may be, a god.

In Italy and Austria the Fool goes by the name Mat, which is really an Arabic word, meaning 'a dead person'. Gérard Rijnberk thinks this name has been given to the Fool as one who is dead to reason. However, it could also refer to one who is dead to this world. This card undoubtedly marks the finish of one cycle and the beginning of a new; in other words it is, as Jean Chaboseau remarks, an indication of the return to unity, of the Spirit to its source. And, I would add, in a cosmic sense it gives an intimation of involution as opposed to evolution, the commencement of a period of *Pralaya* (dissolution or rest) after one of *Manvantara* (manifestation). Which recalls to mind Einstein's expanding and contracting Universe.

This card pictures that 'death and danger dog the heels of worth'. We are not, however, 'fools by heavenly compulsion'. Clearly the

Fool (in the highest sense of this card) has
caught the echo of Browning's words:

> Fool! All that is, at all,
> Lasts ever past recall;
> Earth changes, but thy soul and God stand
> sure:
> What entered into thee,
> *That* was, is, and shall be:
> Time's wheel runs back or stops: Potter and
> clay endure.

CHAPTER TWO

THE MINOR ARCANA

Some authorities think that the Tarot grew out of the *Carte di Baldini*, or Italian Tarocchi cards, wrongly attributed to Andrea Mantegna, which set dates back only to 1470. However, this is unlikely as the Mantegna cards comprised five suits, whereas those of the Minor Arcana (like our modern playing-cards) consist of four. Moreover, the Mantegna cards have very slight relation to the symbolism of Tarot cards as we know them.

On the face of it, therefore, it is more than probable that the Mantegna cards, like our modern playing-cards, evolved from an earlier source, and *this* was the Tarot.

Naturally, in the course of the centuries, and as cards came to be employed more for the purpose of amusement than for divination, many new departures took place. And, not surprisingly, this has led to much confusion on the part of modern investigators who have engaged in the study of comparative symbolism.

A.E. Waite associates the diamond suit of modern playing-cards with the Wands (or

Sceptres) of the Tarot. Hearts he makes
correspond with the Tarot Cups. The club
suit he lines up with the old Tarot Swords;
and Pentacles (or money cards, sometimes
called Deniers) he considers as the
prototypes of our spades.

Pentacle

What is meant by a Pentacle? Originally it
was a material object, generally in the form
of a circle, containing certain magical signs,
the chief of which was an interlaced triangle;
though other signs were added for some
particular purpose. A piece of fine linen or
parchment was sometimes folded with five
corners, and then suitably inscribed with
characters. Worn mostly suspended by a
chain or cord from the neck, and against the
bare skin, as a cross is now by those of the
Greek Church, the Pentacle was supposed to
protect from this or that ill and to bring luck
to its owner. Pentacles were variously devised
for different ends, some being employed by
the magician to control the spirits which he
evoked.

That Waite was wrong in all his inferences
as to the Tarot suits, save that of Cups
corresponding to our hearts, is scarcely open
to doubt. Paul Foster Case differs from him,
in assigning diamonds to Pentacles, the club
suit to Wands, and spades to Swords. Here
he is in agreement with 'Papus' and myself.

But I cannot conform to his view or that of
'Papus' as to the affinities they find between
the four suits and the Elements. 'Papus' and
Case both make the Wand (or Sceptre)
correspond to Fire, and Cup to Water (the
latter being correct). But Case connects the
Pentacle with Earth, and the Sword with
Air; while 'Papus' relates the Sword to
Earth, the Pentacle to Air. I am unable to
accept the ruling of either of them in this
respect.

The Star of David

If we study carefully the secret sign of the
Star of David ✡ it must become immediately
evident that it expresses the synthesis of Fire
and Water. Split up, it consists of the
following parts:

a	△	Fire
b	▲	Air
c	▽	Earth
d	▽	Water

You will note that Fire is opposite Water, Air
opposite Earth; also this arrangement
coincides with that of the symbols for the
Elements in the four hands of the Hindu
deity *Ardhanari*, the Wand (Earth) being
diagonally opposed to the Pentacle (Air),
and the Cup (Water) to the Sword (Fire).
The creatures at the four corners of Card

XXI (the World) likewise symbolize the four Elements.

Elphas Levi, with whom I am at one upon this point, gives the Eagle as Azoth (Air), the Man as Mercury (Water), the Lion as Sulphur (Fire), and the Bull as Salt (Earth).

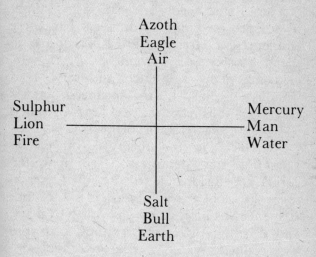

<pre>
                    Azoth
                    Eagle
                    Air

Sulphur   Mercury
Lion   ──────────┼────────── Man
Fire   Water

                    Salt
                    Bull
                    Earth
</pre>

According to the Vedanta, the elements are Light or Fire, Air, Water, and Earth; these being respectively, the World of Brahma, Casual World, Subtle World, and Gross World. Aristotle's elements were in the same order. The elements play a very important part in Mahayana Buddhism. In Tibet, China, and Japan little devices (*stupas*) are put above graves on the anniversary of a person's death. At the base of these devices is a cube, representing earth; above this is a sphere for water; next is a triangle standing for fire; and finally a crescent betokens the element of air. This latter may be taken to be the primordial substance in which manifestation first takes place. In all of these sequences water precedes earth.

There has been, and still is, a great divergence of opinion with regard to these emblematic figures on Card XXI, and as to their correct correspondence with the elements. Now a French authority, Jean Chaboseau, has, I am convinced, in his recently published work *Le Tarot*, provided us with the key to this problem.

He refers to the theory advanced by Lucretius, and doubtless based upon the earlier conclusions of Anaximander, that in the process of Creation the origin of the other elements was Fire; which gave birth to gases, and these to Air. Heat breathing forth into Air produced Water; this slowly coagulated, thus forming all solid matter along with the Earth.

Sequence of Symbols

Now, if we examine Card XXI of the Major Arcana in the light of this key, we shall see that the Lion, standing for Fire, is the true starting-point in the sequence of symbols. The Eagle comes next, representing Air; this is followed by the Man, for Water; and lastly the Ox, Earth. It therefore becomes clear

that those who make the Man correspond to
Air are in error, this element being rightly
related to the Eagle. If it be argued that the
latter properly belongs to Scorpio, it may be
remarked that the Scales and Scorpio formed
one sign with the Latins before Augustus; the
Scales being then the claws of the Scorpion:
and the Scales is an airy sign.

Further, to persist, as some do, that
Aquarius does not symbolize Water is to
ignore the fact that the root of Aquarius is
Aqua, the Latin for water. Minerva (Pallas
Athene) was, to quote Dr Oskar Scyffert, 'the
clear, transparent æther, whose purity is
always breaking forth in unveiled brilliancy
through the clouds that surround it.' The
birds mostly associated with her are the owl,
because of her wisdom; and the cock, owing
to her warlike propensities. But she was
supposed to have sprung from the brain of
Jupiter, therefore the eagle (symbol of the
Divine Breath, perpetual motion) also
belongs to her.

One must bear in mind that the
astrological signs of the zodiac have no actual
agreement with the astronomical
constellations. The latter are always
gradually shifting their position with regard
to the earth, so that in the stage before the
rise of Babylon (about 5000-2800 B.C.) the
sun stood in the zodiacal sign called the
Twins (Gemini). The names of the months

were originally indicated by their meteorological conditions; thus the rain season was symbolized by Capricornus, Aquarius, and Pisces.

It is an interesting fact that Ninib (Saturn) preserved water attributes; the first-born of Ea, he was known as 'lord of wells and of the sea', and 'opener of wells'. Ea, the Babylonian water god, was represented as carrying a vase of water and standing upon a capricorn (not originally a goat, but the sea-monster *Hippocampus guttalaus*). As Aquarius follows Capricorn, and is governed by Saturn, Ea was evidently the first-named; there was at that time no idea, in the minds of most people, as to Aquarius (Ea) having any relation to Air. The ancients – and even such philosophers as Empedocles, in somewhat more modern times – thought of water, fire, air, and earth, astrologically, actually as such; very few meant by such terms, as astrologers now do, just qualities.

Still, in these days, as of old, the true inner signification of the signs of the zodiac is little understood. While we are discussing the elements, it may be pointed out that in the account of the flood given in the Bible, the rain falling from heaven relates to Aquarius; the waters upon the face of the earth to Pisces; and the subsiding of the water, with the appearance of dry land, to Aries. This sequence of events also refers to the descent of Spirit into Matter, the consequent clash of opposites, and thus disharmony; then the commencement of the return journey from Matter, of Spirit to its source. As the rain comes from above, it is obvious that Air must take precedence of Water; though some cartomancers would have it the other way round.

In almost all parts of the world are to be found the four classes indicated by the symbols of the four suits of the Minor Arcana; there are in India, for instance, the *Brahmans* or Priests (Cups), *Kshetriyas* or Warriors (Swords), *Vaisyas* or Merchants (Pentacles), and *Sudras* or Labourers (Wands). Obviously the Cup, Goblet, or chalice refers to the Priest: it must be associated with the element of Water; the Spade (*spatha*, or two-edged sword) stands for the Soldier; also as a consequence should be related to the element of Fire; the Pentacle is the emblem of the constantly changing nature of Money, which circulates everywhere, as does the Air; and, finally, the Wand is the cudgel of the Peasant, as also the sceptre of the King: the symbol of power in respect of earth. As the Pentacle is the circle of the heavens, so our Diamonds symbolize the four points of the compass.

It should be borne in mind that the Eagle has always been associated with Jupiter; who, the sungod of Heliopolis, dwelt upon

Olympus in the region of the upper air. The Man, on the other hand, fits in with Hermes: the cupbearer of the gods, who was continually travelling to and from earth and heaven, and formed the link between the gods and mankind; just as Christ does between God and humanity. Hermes is the same as Thoth of the Egyptians; he whose name means Logos, or 'the Word'.

Thus the symbolism of the Man (on Card XXI) appears to have a direct bearing upon the Holy Grail, the Eucharist, and the chalice of the clergy. As rain falls on earth, to rise again heavenward; similarly the spirit descends to earth, later to return to its source. Hokmah, correctly the third Sephira, is termed the Logos and the First Born; is, according to the Qabalah, 'The Only Begotten Son', and is on the Tree of Life at the angle of the Man (Aquarius). By the way, Aquarius was so called because at that time of the year the Nile overflowed its banks, and was thus the promise of an abundant harvest and fresh life.

The Winged Man
Why, one may ask, is the Man on the twenty-first card of the Major Arcana given wings? Here we see a connection again with Mercury (or the Greek Hermes), who has winged sandals or *talaria*; wings, on his *petasus* or broad-brimmed hat, and *caduceus* or

staff. We can take it that the rod itself symbolizes the material element; the entwined serpents about it, the vital breaths and the spiritual or fiery element; the wings at its summit, the airy one; whilst in his capacity of cupbearer, the fourth, the watery element, needs no pictoral representation. By the wand, we are reminded of the oak under which the Druids worshipped, the symbol of perishable matter; whereas the mistletoe, growing upon its trunk was, like the snakes on the rod, emblematic of eternal Spirit.

All this symbolism indicates quite clearly that whoever devised the symbolism of these cards was of a spiritual-minded and highly intellectual type. Waite argues that 'allegory and symbolism are catholic – of all centuries, nations and times; they are not more Egyptian than Mexican; they are of Europe and Cathay, of Tibet beyond the Himalayas and of the London gutters. As allegory and symbol, the cards correspond to many types of ideas and things; they are universal and not particular.' But is it true to say they are 'of the London gutters'? Such a criticism does not throw a ray of light upon the mystery of the wisdom enshrined in these cards. For it goes without saying that in bygone days, when there was no well-educated and vast reading public as now, the man in the street had no knowledge of such allegory any more than had the average

Egyptian of the hieratic writing.

Anyone who starts to make a serious study of the Tarot will very soon find that writers upon the subject frequently take unwarranted liberties with the cards, are a law unto themselves; they are at variance often upon points about which there can be no question of doubt. Even Gérard van Rijnberk, who in his excellent work *Le Tarot* has spared himself no pains and is generally accurate, errs in stating that there are 95 cards in a Michiate or Florentine pack, whereas it actually consists of 97. This is an augmented Tarot, as the Bolognese is a diminished one; the latter comprising 62 cards in all, cards 2, 3, 4, and 5 of the Minor Arcana being omitted. These two are doubtless attempts at 'perfected' Tarots. I am, however, content to accept the Tarot as I find it, to reproduce as nearly as can be what I believe to be the original symbolism with the right interpretations. The Tarot is so near to perfection it has no need of such embellishments. All of the chief figures in a Minchiate pack face one, and there are five suits instead of four. 'Trappola', the first game of cards which seems to have been known to the Italians, was played with a pack of 36 cards.

CHAPTER THREE

DIVINATION BY THE TAROT

For those of us who are unable to read the *Akashic* records with any degree of clearness, and very few can, it is impossible either to prove or disprove that there is any truth in the ancient and persistent belief that Tubal-Cain invented the anvil, Moses the trumpet, Hermes Trismegistus draughts, the Lydians tennis, Dædalus the axe and awl, and Palamedes chess.

Similarly, one cannot positively prove or disprove the quaint theory advanced by some that the Devil, in his spare time (and he cannot have had much leisure at his disposal), invented playing-cards; and, as the ancestors of all cards – the Tarot. Were such indeed the case, then Satan performed thereby a good service to mankind. For cards have constantly provided harmless entertainment to countless millions, while the Tarot has been of continual and far deeper benefit to humanity.

Perhaps, despite Pope's moralizing, there are worse epitaphs than 'A youth of frolics, and old age of cards.' Much depends upon the nature of one's youthful frolics, as also the use made of the cards, one scarcely need remark.

A Chinese seventeenth century dictionary states that playing-cards were invented five hundred years before for the amusement of the concubines of the Sung emperor Suan-Ho. Edmund Dulac, that outstanding authority upon playing-cards, has mentioned that a card found by Von le Coq near Tarfan, among Wigour manuscripts, an undoubted Chinese card, must be taken to date back no later than the eleventh century. 'In the East,' as Dulac says, 'playing-cards are the most delightful things imaginable, from the delicate miniatures of kings, viziers, elephants, and so forth, and the various emblems that Persia shares with India, to the simpler woodcut patterns of China and Japan. All these cards have suits with court cards or trumps, and have in common with the Tarot devices the swords and the Moon or money symbol, to which may be added the bamboos and circles of Mah-jong, which is, after all, only a card game played with tiles instead of pasteboards.'

Pack Variations

The symbols of the four suits of the Minor Arcana vary in different countries. In the common Spanish pack the devices Wands or Sceptres, Cups, Swords, and Pentacles still survive. They become in the German Tarot (which is, by the way, a very bad one), hearts, acorns, hawk-bells, and leaves. However, in the French and subsequently in the English pack, clubs, hearts, spades, and diamonds were substituted for the original devices. One small point intimating that in earlier times the Spade suit was definitely associated with that of Swords is that, in an English pack brought out in 1790 by Rowley & Co., the King of Spades is represented by Louis XVI, king of France; and in the top left-hand corner of this card is shown a short two-edged sword.

It has been suggested that the Tarot cards evolved from an ancient form of chess. One might, though, quite as reasonably conclude that chess evolved from the Tarot. Whether the cards came from India, Egypt, or China, reached Italy first from the last-mentioned, were introduced into the West from the East by the crusaders or Arabs, or arrived in Europe with the Gipsies, is of little moment. What is of far more importance than the age of the cards is the antiquity of much of their symbolism. As to this, at least, there can be no divergence of opinion.

Divination

Although it is impossible in the confines of a book to give instruction on the use of the Tarot for divination, I will now give a reading of a Tarot spread from the 'Great

Pack' – that is to say, the Major and Minor Arcana combined. Those who are interested in this aspect of the Tarot can obtain full information from the Insight Institute, which also supplies the Tarot cards.

Not to make things too complicated, then, let us limit the lay-out to six cards. This is not a made-up spread, with the cards picked out to suit the problem, but an actual one sent to me for interpretation.

A wife and mother finds herself in a puzzling situation, the necessity to make a choice between three courses of action. She has to decide whether to go and take up her abode permanently with her elder son; to make her home with her younger son in Trinidad, and to help look after and train his children; or to rejoin her husband, who is in Ceylon, and from whom she has been separated by the war. Not knowing what to do, she decided to consult the cards for some indication as to how she ought to act. The cards, in the order in which they should be read, from left to right, were as follows:

XIX	IV	V	VI	XII	XVII
The Sun	Emperor	Pope	Lovers	Hanged Man	Star

The Pope and the Lovers must receive close attention; for they are the middle cards upon which the problem, as a whole, turns. These cards are right to the point, as the Pope indicates the need for the consultant to

do what she feels, from a conscientious point
of view, to be the correct thing, and also
refers to reunion; while the Lovers (Card VI)
stresses her state of indecision.

The Sun, at the commencement of the lay-
out, shows that the querent's outlook is a
bright one; she is doubtless of a cheerful
disposition and has looked upon the sunny
side of things in the past. As this card is
followed immediately by the Emperor, which
card stands for completion (and in the case of
a woman may have reference to marriage),
and, furthermore, the Sun tells of 'Paradise
regained', it is clear that the consultant's
thoughts are directed chiefly towards her
husband, whom she hopes to rejoin. While
the Hanged Man gives intimation that, being
a mother as well as a wife, she will have to
make some personal sacrifices, the future, as
indicated by Card XVII, looks for her fairly
bright.

The Star stands for *selflessness and spiritual
love*. However, since the light of the Star is
only a reflection of that of the Sun, at the
start of the spread, it appears as though some
of the brightness will go out of the
consultant's life by her doing what she
recognizes to be her duty.

Let us now add up the digits of the cards
and see what information we can obtain from
their numbers in combination. The numbers
of the whole line of cards add up to 63 = 9,

which is the number of the Hermit, so the consultant will have to act with caution and face the obstacles in her path by the light of her clear understanding. As the first and last cards of the spread add up to 36, which also reduces to 9, the need for prudence is stressed. Cards IV and V likewise reduce to 9, as do the *Lovers* and *Hanged Man*.

The *Pope* and *Lovers* add up to 11 = 2, intimating that the querent will have to employ her critical faculty and keep a guard upon her speech, as she may find that her husband is strong-minded and inclined to dominate her, perhaps because he has grown accustomed to leading his own life and having his own way. The last two cards again reduce to 11 =2; and so we can conclude that, as the *Star* follows the *Hanged Man*, it is by selflessness and the exercise of spiritual love that she will gain peace and a large degree of happiness in her reunion with her husband.

Of course, as I have previously remarked, one could obtain a more detailed reading by having cards of both the Major and Minor Arcana; but one must not keep on laying out spreads for the solution of the same problem. By this means one would, ultimately, be sure to get a reading to one's own satisfaction. However, one cannot alter one's fate by thus badgering fortune. If one desires to gain the greatest advantage by consulting the cards, then one should set about planning one's future wisely, for we are none of us really slaves to circumstances. The cards, like the stars, can give us good advice, but they cannot compel us to act in one way or another. We must not make the Tarot, any more than the Sun, the Moon, and the Stars, guilty of our disasters; as though all our misfortunes are brought upon us 'by a divine thrusting on'.

A Glimpse Ahead

People often ask me how is it possible that such inanimate things as cards, small pieces of paste-board, can enable one to read the future. My answer is that one has to accept in this life a vast number of things which one cannot explain: space, for instance; how the celestial bodies are kept in their appointed courses; by what means mind, which is invisible and intangible, can control the movements of the physical body.

There is no sense in denying that something happens, just because one's very limited intelligence cannot account for it. The other day, when I was waiting in a queue I noticed a man standing behind me with a book under his arm. I asked him if he would mind telling me if the book was Du Maurier's *Peter Ibbetson*, and he replied that it was. The book was a new copy evidently bought from a shop, and the last time I read that novel was several years ago, when I borrowed it from my local library.

Now how did I know that he had that particular work of fiction, *Peter Ibbetson*, under his arm? The only possible explanation seems to be that one's thoughts sometimes reach out and pick up what is in another person's mind. A feasible solution as to how one can get a glimpse of the probable future from the cards is that they fall into line with and picture much of what lies concealed in the depths of the subconscious mind, which can look further back and ahead than the normal waking consciousness.

Be that as it may, the fact remains, as anyone can soon prove for himself, that the Tarot does afford us a glimpse of the likely trend of events. I say *likely* advisedly, for there is nothing in the least fatalistic about the Tarot. Man can become, like the *Juggler*, master of his own fate, if he 'plays the cards' rightly. Were this not so, then there would be very little purpose in consulting the cards, the main object of which is to avoid falling into errors which one might otherwise make.

We are all trying constantly to look ahead, in our business undertakings, the way we speculate with our money, choose our friends, and enter into marriage partnerships. One might just as well do deliberately and according to some system, with one's eyes open, what one usually does in a muddled and blind manner. There is no reason why we should not use every faculty and means we possess to shape our lives more wisely. And the Tarot will assist us to do this.

The superior person will no doubt dismiss the practice of cartomancy as mere superstition. But that one man's belief is another man's heresy, and *vice versa*, is a truism so manifest that it hardly needs stating. One must not conclude that, because so-called superstitions are more the outcome of intution and emotions than of careful reasoning, they are therefore without the least foundation and are entirely false.

Feeling exists prior to deliberative thought, the babe turns instinctively to its mother for nourishment long before its mentality has developed. Reason must always be the servant of intuition, just as science must be the handmaid of religion — can never rob faith of its inner, unquenchable light. Of course, there are always those (the dogs of Hecate) who would howl down the stars, and for them this book will be as dust upon the desert.

One use to which the Tarot can be put is to aid us to see into the secret depths of the soul. How much is mirrored from without into the mind, how much reflected from within outward, it is not easy to decide. We can obtain a clearer understanding of our true nature by reading the cards, which will serve as pointers to what lies concealed below the surface of our waking consciousness. They can, therefore, to some extent, help us to discover our weaknesses, prejudices, and proneness to this or that error. Rightly used, they can perform the function of a psycho-therapeutic agent.

We see from the last card of the Major Arcana, that man must learn that Wisdom is the twin brother of Folly. In short, the Fool at his best has reached the stage when he realizes that he is All – and Nothing. 'Thou art man, Thou art woman, Thou art boys, Thou art girls, Thou art an old man tottering on his stick,' says the *Svetasvatan Upanishad*. 'Thou art created with thy face turning on all sides ... Thou art the stormy cloud, the seas, the seasons. Thou art without beginning. Thou art infinite, Thou, from whom proceed all universes.' So man can, as Plato remarks in his *Timoeus*, 'after having attained his health and integrity, recover the luminous path of his pristine state.'

What is called for today is less calculation and more imagination – a Renascence of Wonder. We must constantly bear in mind that the road through *this* life, symbolized by the Major Arcana, leads but to a higher one. If you are wise you will 'hitch your wagon to a star' (Card XVII), turning your eyes like those of the Hanged Man heavenwards. *Sic itur ad astra*. The Tarot points the way.

INDEX

Acca Larentia, 20
air, 74, 75, 76, 77, 78, 79
Aries, 78
Aleph, 14
Amrita, 56
Anaximander, 76
Angel of Time, 44-7
  see also Temperance
Aquarius, 77, 80
ankh, 21
Anubis, 35
Apollonius of Tyana, 34
Artemis, 20
Astraea, 31
Atlanteans, 59
Atropos, 36
Atout cards, 13
  see also trump cards
Atys, 41
Ayin, 13
Azoth, 75

The Balance, 30-2
Beth, 16
The Black Magician, 47-50, 55
Boaz, 16
Book of Thoth, 16
Browning, 37, 48, 71
bull, 75, 76

cancer, 31, 56
Carte di Baldini, 72
Case, Paul Foster, 29, 31, 40, 50, 73, 74
Ceres, 21
Chaboseau, Jean, 16, 41, 70, 76
The Chariot, 26-30
Chesed, 31
Choice of Hercules, 25
Christ, 43, 80
  see also Jesus
christianity, 25
Cos, 25
crocodiles, 69
cups, 7, 73, 74, 79

The Day of Judgement, 63-5
Death, 42-4
Demeter, 21
Devil, 48, 49
Diana, 17
Divine, Dr George, 50
Divine Impulsion, 26
Divine Justice, 30, 51
Divine Law, 15
Divine Light, 62, 65
Dulac, Edmund, 84
dyaus, 17

Ea, 78
Eagle, 75, 76, 77, 79
earth, 74, 75, 76
The Emperor, 21-2, 87
The Empress, 17-21
The Enchantress, 37-40
Eternal Life, symbol of, 15, 31
Eternal Spirit, 26

'female Pope', 16
    see also The High Priestess
Fire, 74, 75, 76
The Fool, 8, 9, 13, 22, 67-71, 92
fortune-telling, 10

Gabriel, 30
Gaea, 17
gammadion, 64
Gautama Buddha, 34
Geburah, 31
de Givry, Grillot, 42
Goethe, 58
The 'Great Balance', 30

Harding, M. Esher, 20
The Hanged Man, 40-2, 66, 87, 88
Havamal, 42
Hearts, 73
Hebe, 55
Hecate, 57, 91
Hercules, 25
Hermanubis, 35
Hermes, 80
Hermes Trismegistus, 34

The Hermit, 32-4, 62, 67, 69
Herodotus, 59
The High Priestess, 15-17, 23, 28, 50

Insight Institute, 21, 25, 34, 51, 52, 54, 58, 61, 86
Ishtar, 19, 20
Isis, 15, 19
Ixion, 34

Jakin, 16
Jerger, Français, 53
Jesus, 42
    see also Christ
Judaeus, Philo, 56
The Juggler, 13, 14-15, 22, 31, 32, 47, 48, 67
Jupiter, 77, 79
Justice, 30

Koran, 53, 57, 63

Labours of Hercules, 36, 38, 40
Lachesis, 36
Lamed, 42
Lares, 20
Lemuria, 58
Leo, 40
Lévi, Eliphas, 34, 62, 75
Libra, 31, 40
The Lightning-Struck Tower, 50-3
Lion, 75, 76

The Lovers, 25-6, 86, 87, 88
Lucifer, 35, 48
Lucretius, 76

Ma, 58, 59
Maat, 30
Macrocosm, 66
Magus, 22, 28, 30, 47
man, 75, 76, 77, 80
Mantegna, Andrea, 72
Mars, 39
'Mat', 70
Maxwell, 41
Maya, 43, 67
Memorabilia, 26
Mendes, 49
Mercury, 75, 80
Mercy, 31
Merope, 54
Mesmer, 47
Microcosm, 66
The Moon, 56-61, 89
Moralia, De Facie in Orbe Lunae, 37
Morley, H.T., 23, 45
Mu, 58

Nephthys, 21
Nirvana, 41

Odin, 42
Orpheus, 65
Osiris, 16, 23, 30, 34, 36, 56

Pagad, 14, 37
Pan, 49

Papus, 16, 23, 26, 28, 29, 31, 33, 38, 44, 57, 73, 74
Pentacles, 7, 73-4, 79
Pisces, 78
Plato, 92
Pleiades, 54
Plutarch, 37, 69
The Pope, 22-5, 32, 83, 86
Prodicus, 25
The Psychology of Everyman, 50

Qabalah, 13, 80

The Reaper, 42-4, 47
Reichenbach, 47
van Rijnberk, Gerard, 16, 24, 70, 82
Rowley and Co., 85

Sahu, 56
salt, 75
Satan, 15, 35, 49, 53, 83
Saturn, 78
scales, 77
Scorpio, 77
Scyffert, Dr Oskar, 77
Set, 21, 35
Sisyphus, 54
Smaragdine Tablet, 37
smriti, 23
Solomon's Temple, 16
sphinx, 35
sruti, 23
The Star, 53-6, 87, 88
Star of David, 74-6

sulphur, 75
The Sun, 61-2, 87, 89
Swords, 7, 73, 74, 79

Tammuz, 20
'Tarocchi cards', 72
Le Tarot, 76, 82
Temperance, 44-7
    see also Angel of Time
Thoth, 30
Thummim, 29
Timoeus, 92
Tiphereth, 31
Tora, 15, 28, 58, 66
'Tree of Life', 10
Trump cards, 13
    see also Atout cards
Typhon, 35

Uranus, 17
Urikittu, 20
Urim, 29

Virgo, 31, 40

Waite, A.E., 8, 26, 28, 72, 73, 81
Wands, 7, 72, 74, 79
Water, 74, 76, 77, 78, 79
'Water of Life', 19
Wheel of Fortune, 34-7
The Winged Man, 80-82
Woman's Mysteries, 20
The World, 65-7

Xenophon, 26

Zeus, 17